I live in Stirling, Scotland, which is a truly beautiful part of the world, surrounded by hills and countryside. I only started writing poetry in recent years as a way to relax and record some of my life experiences to pass on to my children. I enjoy reading mostly fantasy fiction when I have time, which is difficult as I also work full time and volunteer with a local Community First Responder group as well as being a wife, mother and grandmother.

To Patricia I hope
you enjoy reading this
book. Best wishes
Liz Gillespie
x

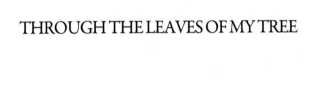

THROUGH THE LEAVES OF MY TREE

Liz Gillespie

THROUGH THE LEAVES OF MY TREE

Vanguard Press

VANGUARD PAPERBACK

© Copyright 2016
Liz Gillespie
Cover illustration by David Crossley, Crossley Custom Inc.

The right of Liz Gillespie to be identified as author of
this work has been asserted by her in accordance with the
Copyright, Designs and Patents Act 1988.

All Rights Reserved

No reproduction, copy or transmission of this publication
may be made without written permission.
No paragraph of this publication may be reproduced,
copied or transmitted save with the written permission of the publisher, or
in accordance with the provisions
of the Copyright Act 1956 (as amended).

Any person who commits any unauthorised act in relation to
this publication may be liable to criminal
prosecution and civil claims for damages.

A CIP catalogue record for this title is
available from the British Library.

ISBN 978 1 90755 288 5

Vanguard Press is an imprint of
Pegasus Elliot MacKenzie Publishers Ltd.
www.pegasuspublishers.com

First Published in 2016

Vanguard Press
Sheraton House Castle Park
Cambridge England

Printed & Bound in Great Britain by CMP (uk) Limited

This book is dedicated to all my friends and family who encouraged me to write, submit and are now saying, "I told you so…" and to my wonderful husband who supports me through all my adventures no matter how bizarre and amazing they turn out to be.

Author's Note

A collection of stories and memories expressed in verse.

This little book was never meant for publication, just for me to write down my memories in verse.
I have always enjoyed playing with words and started writing them thinking I could do much better than some of even the more famous published poets but if I am being honest with myself... I don't think they are all that great. Saying that though, my poems mean a lot to me, they not only help me remember things I have done, places I have visited or things that my friends and I have seen but I thought it would be a nice thing to pass it on to the ones I love after I am gone.

I tried to keep my poems secret but as time went on more people have found out that I write them and for some reason wanted to read them along with any new ones I pen and so inspiring me to write more and to persuade me to produce this little book.

I would like to thank everyone who inspired and encouraged me to continue writing and sharing my stories and poems when I did not believe they were that good. Who knows you may even be the subject of one of them.

Through the Leaves of My tree

Sunshine sparkles through the leaves of my tree
Shadows of my neighbours bounce by in a blink of an eye
Birds chirp out their happy little song and others echo near by

Warm air sighs through the leaves of my tree
Sounds like whispered secrets from the sky
Birds chirp out their happy little song and others echo near by

A ribbon of light escapes through the leaves of my tree
Making a warm pool of grass in which I now lay
Birds chirp out their happy little song and others echo near by

Spring time

As the day breaks creatures stir from their slumber
To a glorious sight to behold and ponder

From the silence of the night the bird song starts
A rising crescendo when you're up with the larks

Skies morph from a sparkling inky blue
To pinks and oranges reflected in the morning dew

A dusky glow to a dazzling sight
We wake from our sleep to brilliant day light

Winter ends

A lacy curtain of frost creeps up the window pane
icicles hang down like pendant gems from the overhangs

A crisp carpet crunches under foot as I hurry down the lane
the warm breath streaming from my mouth is grasped by the
cold night hands

A winter sun reflecting off the newly laid snow
snowdrops emerge in a bid to announce spring time is just
around the corner

Pendant gems drip into a thousand little puddles on the ground
the sun breaks through the icy fog to make the earth relax in a
warmer dawn

In The Garden

Fermenting, mulching, morphing into something new
Digging, hoeing, feeding shoots of life that sprout from the
garden stew

Nurture, encouraging, creating new life from the earthy mound
Digging harvesting collecting the fruit from the carefully
tended ground

Black Velvet

Dark as the night with velvety fur
Mischievous and fun there is no stopping her
She darts through the door to see who is home
Looking to play she won't leave you alone

Bouncing through the house on her own little mission
Taking over your lap no need for permission
A playmate is required and you have a look see
As she bounces on the head of a sleepy Cookie

The toys lay around but no interest is paid
A live victim is required the challenge is made
A squat, a wiggle, a pounce from the ground
Movement so swift and not even a sound

A tumble of fur all over the floor
A success full ambush then exit the door
Fun is all over as quick as a flash
Cookie now knows it is safe to relax

Coorie up

Fear ye not my fine feathered friend
The wind blow south and in tae watter you will end
Coorie up and batten down, the nicht will be long and drawn
But fear ye not my fine feathered friend it will be richt by the
morning dawn

Tour Separation

The sun yawned and stretched into another new dawn
thoughts of the day ahead silenced the empty ringing in my
heart

A thousand miles away the day is already in full swing
and that same sun revengefully scorches the land that keeps us
apart

I count the minutes as they slowly race by eager to reach the
finish line
a line that longs to scream… welcome home
and silences the empty ringing in my heart

Autumn

Golden yellow, orange, red and brown
Sun burnt leaves fall gently to the ground
Trees shed their leaves to a thick carpet below
And late summer flowers put on one last show

The season now changes as the hot summer cools
Woodlands are filling with fungi and toadstools
Days grow much shorter and the warm air chills
And a light dusting of frost tops some nearby hills

People wrapped up with scarf, gloves and hat
Hibernating animals have a good layer of fat
Berries ripen in the hedgerows all around
And squirrels hide their nuts where they can later be found

The Lavender Lady

The Lavender Lady is a person I know well
A friendly wee wifey with a story to tell
She writes little rhymes in a book she keeps hidden
so nobody sees the verse she has written

The Lavender Lady is funny and bright
I love to spend time with her it's always a delight
You never quite know what she will do next
Sometimes she is lovely and sometimes a wee pest

The Lavender Lady has a hippyish flair
With long mental skirts and dark purple hair
She sips on mint tea from noon until night
And bakes lots of cakes that are such a delight

The Conference

The team has assembled we each take our chair
Mr Sinclair is present and of course Mrs Blair

Attendance is thin and a few more no shows
The only CFATA is Mr Stokoe!

The conference starts, agendas laid out
The tension is mounting no time to hang about

We have discussed all our figures, our courses and stats
Pleased with ourselves and self-pats on our backs

We discuss all the training and what needs to be done
The competitions we missed and the awards we had not won

A promise that next year we will turn up the heat
On that final note we rise to our feet

Words

Words are sometimes not enough to express what needs to be said
Some things take time to get it right and put the matter right to bed
So many times we jump so far and the conclusions are all wrong
The song sheets from which we all sing are just a different song

To rush head long without a check is a silly thing to do
False-hoods, often matter of fact, when what we said is true
Respect and trust are fragile things and cast aside with ease
and many people come across as extremely hard to please

A tunnel vision blinkered view by narrow minded twits
with snippy mails, sarcastic quotes and horrid little quips
lets take a view just for a change from a few steps further out
and have some trust in what you see from within and the world about

Who Will Hold Me

Who will hold me when I am feeling low
When I am feeling sad and have lost my glow
Who will hold me when I am feeling blue
When you're not around and I think of you

I am always here, it's expected of me
A shoulder to cry on and a friendly ear
I will solve all your problems and give you a hug
I won't laugh at you or suggest a new drug

Who will listen when I am down
When I have problems and there's no one around
Who will hold me and say it's okay
When you're not around and life looks so grey

I am here come rain or come shine
To help and support anyone at anytime
I will offer you cake and wipe away your tears
I will listen to your tale and help combat your fears

Dinosaur

There's a dinosaur sitting in our office who objects to anything new
He refuses to answer to anyone and only talks to a privileged few

His policies are so outdated and he seems permanently stuck in the past
He's been in there for quite some time now and he thinks he is going to last!

Do you think he will listen to the youngsters whose ideas are new and in tune?
There is a dinosaur sitting in our office and I hope he leaves us quite soon!

Pirate Party

They arrive in their hordes aligning the step
A group of wee pirates looking just like Mr Depp
For treasure they seek and ashore they have come
Armed with some swords, a blankee and a gun

They pile in the house and abandon their wellies
And head for the table adorned with food, cake and jellies
Treasure piled high in the midst of it all
They stand there agog mouths opened in awe

Laid out on the left is the cake of a tale
A once treasured ship that was eaten by a whale
On the right was a barrel of the captain's finest rum
And standing to starboard was me nan and me mum

After taking their fill of the cake and the rum
And a wee one's asleep sucking on her thumb
The sugar kicks in as nan makes herself tea
I think one has found a squealing banshee

Over the noise a yell "oooo come all and see"
Papa has got himself a brand new Wii
I want to play Super Mario but the girls win with Let's Dance
The music is cranked up and they all start to prance

Ten kids move in time to the guide on the screen
All kinds of music from rock and techno to Abba's Dancing
Queen
At five p.m. they all start to go
Stuffed full and tired out they can't cope with no more

Trial of the Soup

A creamy vegetable soup was called to trial one winters day
The charges against the creamy broth were numerous you may
say

Its cheek and insubordination surpassed the accepted norm
It lingered with intent to keep its presence safe and warm

A waxy cardboard cup was where it waited for its chance
And from its murky depths it would just insult anyone who'd
glance

The council for the defence declared its not its fault m'lord
Its life has been filled with drink and drugs and the odd psycho
ward

The evidence is clear, the jury heard, as they listened to what
was said
No drink or drugs had been involved just some seasoning and
a herb

So herbs were used, and we must act, to protect us from its
wrath
We cannot allow this soup to insult everyone it sees to pass

It's not its fault it's a vegetable broth, and discriminated
against each day
It's not its fault that society thinks its kind should be locked
away

I appeal your decision for consumption sir, and as you can clearly see
It's terminally ill your grace, the jury, it has mutated splits in its pea

So you're saying it is mentally unsound and it's no fault of its own
You're saying it knows not what it does and is a child in an adult form

The treatment it has suffered sir is almost inhumane
And I urge you sir to release it sir from consumption by the drain

The discrimination act m'lord for those so cruelly afflicted
And the human rights of this poor soup has been just horridly restricted

The judge considered the evidence from the honourable Sir Sinclair
And the jury briefed so carefully so they are fully aware

The foreman rose with a glance at the soup let out a soulful sigh
The soup is innocent he read aloud and should never been brought to trial

Mother

Tap tap tap goes the Morse code on my leg
The little one has woken and wants to be fed
His empty bottle in hand and a pleading look in his eye
He points to the fridge and lets out a wee sigh

Afternoon nap a chance to catch up
A cuppa tea first and then I won't stop
All too quickly after putting him to bed
The morse code tapping starts again on my leg

Play time begins and his face is a picture
Proud of his creation, a beautiful... Errr... creature
Night garden people are all now in bed
And he taps out his agreement with Morse code on my leg

All shiny and clean and so snugly and soft
My son has his blanky and heads for his cot
Peacefully sleeping wrapped up in his bed
I am already missing his Morse code on my leg

Basic First Aid

Hands all fully gloved and bandages held aloft
The cadets are ready to pounce at as much as a cough

The skills have been inputted like programming a computer
Ready to practice the skills just taught by their tutor

Eager to please and to get it right first time
The wait and then they pounce shouting "This victim is MINE"

A flurry of activity they were taught by the master
And insist on field dressings when all they need is a plaster

A mummified casualty now lies on the floor
And pleased with their efforts they now head out the door

The Dive

The break of dawn, we stretch we yawn, and pack up our mask
and our fins
All loaded up, in the back of the truck, excited about our next
swim
At the site we arrive, we feel so alive, and our adventure that
lays right ahead
All kitted up, from the back of the truck, to the entry point we
are all led

The water looks cold, but were feeling bold as the sun starts to
warm up the rock
A giant stride in, on our faces a grin, and we brace ourselves
for the short drop
Our BCD is inflated, and our belts are all weighted, we enter
with an exciting small splash
Surrounded by bubbles, our hearing is muffled, and to the
surface we rise with a dash

On the surface together, no matter the weather, we signal we
are ready to go
Our kit is all checked, we are to dive on a wreck, located thirty
meters below
A decent to the sea floor, not far from the shore, the fish gather
around for a look
A variety of plant and stuff that has sunk and a signal to check
in a nook

We are all shown the direction and we move in a section away from the rock and the land

The reef falls away, someone spotted a ray and signals the group with his hand

A nice shoal of bream another has seen and a cuttlefish eating his dinner

A fireworm or two has come into view and the photographer changes his filter

A quick check we're all here, the way forward is clear as we descend through the thermal below

The water it shimmers and surrounds all the swimmers as the temperature starts to get cold

From the bow to the hull with air tanks half full, the signal is clear please don't linger

A quick peek inside where an eel chose to hide and almost snaps off my wee finger

We fin to the shore eager for more and forage around in the warm shallows

Small fish all around and look what we found a nubi tucked into a hollow

We wait to get out and while bobbing about we excitedly discuss the whole dive

We strip down to our skin remove wet neoprene feeling enthused and alive

Catching up

Relaxing in your hammock on a warm spring evening
Its vivid colours reflecting the sun setting sky above

Conversation gently folds its arms around me
As I listen to the day's events discussed by the ones I love

The warm breeze carries your neighbour's conversations
through the air
And mixes it gently into the soup of the setting sun

Smiles and laughter each one of us impatiently waiting to add
our penny's worth
a memory has been born, to be recalled at some distant time to
come

Time stands still and we catch up on so much lost over the
years to life and its events
As we recant our adventures, our battles lost and won

Family time and renewing the bonds forged when we were
children
Strong ties reformed and a promise made in the setting Spanish
sun.

Toothache

A tingle, a fizz then pain sears through my mouth
Disbelief… this is not happening as I think about munch
I queued up for ages just for the assistant to shout
Who's next, can I help can you please order your lunch?

It's not happening I dismiss it and as I start to bite
My mind is playing tricks and my stomach says you're right
The soft brown bread baked fresh that very day
But the pain in my gums says you're not eating that! Nope no way!

The dentists phone rings as she answers my call
An emergency appointment she starts but then a stall…
I am sorry to tell you the only time we have free
Is a week next Monday at quarter to three?

An emergency! Sir I am sorry I <u>had</u> heard
But you can take it or leave it and that's my last word
The dentist has golf four mornings this week
Take three painkillers each evening just before you go to sleep

No need to shout sir that is the best I can do
I believe the chemist may have something to help you
Lotion or potion to apply as you need
Now away and geez peace and go boil yer heid.

Waiting

An empty chair there's no one there
I sit and stare at the empty chair
Alone with my phone
Waiting

The silence breaks a machine awakes
The empty chair is still there
Waiting

Not long now a worried brow
I continue to stare at the empty chair
Waiting

Time ticks by I hear a cry
But no one is there in the empty chair
And still I am waiting

There's a rip in the chair don't suppose they care
Because no one is there to sit in the chair
Waiting

A passer-by they briefly nod "Hi"
They must be elsewhere not filling the chair
And so I continue waiting

Patiently waiting in a room just for waiting
Sitting in one chair with another over there
I stare and wait

I hope she's okay and knows I am there
Baby's on its way - does she know I care
And am sitting there in a chair
Waiting

A flurry of commotion - The doors fly open
It's a girl they announce back through the door they bounce
I smile now I'm not waiting

London

An adventure down south with some of the team
Excitement all round it seems like a dream
One of the gang who's never been there before
Was off like a rocket, the first out of the door

Train was packed out from all walks and wild life
The student, the weirdo, the husband and wife
The kids that run up the length of the train
And knock poor Davy's sunburn WILL YOU STOP! HE IS
IN PAIN!

We find the hotel and quickly unpack
Not much room for a thing not even a swung cat
It's clean and it's cheap what more could you get
Thank goodness our tariff is not the hourly rent

Next food is in order and soon head out the door
But Shirley's insistent she wants to explore
A stroll round the area and down to the Thames
What started out drizzle, a monsoon now descends!

A continental breakfast in the morning for all
Then we go off exploring round the area once more
Kings Cross is a wondrous, busy wee place
Smaller than imagined but packed with every creed, colour
and race

Cadet 150 a Guildhall event,
we come from all over to receive praise for time spent
The lord mayor of London and some high level w-ranks
His Royal Highness Prince Phillip said a few words of thanks

Time to escape all the charm and the smarm
Back to the hotel… Who's tripped the alarm
It was me I'm afraid a wee voice was heard said
Was the steam from the shower his face is pure red

Night Out

Re-written and remixed just for my Hubby (to the tune of Little Donkey)

Little door key little door key
Hiding beneath the front door mat
Gotta keep on crawling onwards up the dirty path

Follow the star tonight
Shining bright – shit it's the front porch light
Follow that star tonight their round ma heid
Where I got smacked in a fight

Little door key little door key
Under the dusty mat
Do you think I can get in wi oot waking the cat

Follow the path and stair
Tipped o'er the cat
Now I am the flair

Let's no waken the wife
Or I'll be oot an ma eer
Sooooo
(joined up to the previous verse but now to the tune of Silent Night)
Silent night
Holy night
Wife's in bed
I'm locked oot here
Round yon back
A will try the ither door
Round yon back
She has booby trapped the floor

(tune of Little Donkey)
Little door key little door key
Removed from under the mat
Gotta keep on grovelling onwards
Te the middle o next year…

Nature

Nature is beautiful and many would agree
Just take a look around and permit your eyes to see
So many delicate creations across our fair land
From forest and woods, hill dale and sand

All God's creatures both great and some small
All shapes and sizes, some short and some tall
But what about the crawlies that creep along the floor
The spider, the bug, the ants and lots more

All of them are beautiful if you just open your eyes
Pay attention to the details in the wings, the shape and size
Watch the way they walk or forage for their food
Watch their different temperaments their habits and their moods

They create new life and survive against the odds
They are all still God's creatures
So please don't trample the poor little sods...

A Thought

A thought of you I'd like to say
Is such a nice way to start the day
A thought of you will help me through
A place I am when feeling blue
A thought of you will make me smile
A thought of you just once in a while

Double R

The infamous brothers arrive on the scene
Ronnie and Reggie look keen, lean and mean
Up to no good when in their domain
Nothing is safe no one will remain

Your personal space is no longer your own
Your time has run out so lower your tone
The boys have arrived and you're stopped in your tracks
The infamous brothers the "Double R" act

Ronnie is watching the lamp just for now
And Reggie is meeking for more meow chow
The perimeter secured they settle down for the night
But Ronnie still watches the living room light

My glass is half empty

My glass is half empty, life sucks and that's true.
I sit here each evening with nothing to do

I sit here each weekend, I sit all on my own
There is no one to talk to and no one to phone

I am bored out my head and I haven't a clue
I don't know what is happening and there is nothing to do

No one has called me from the usual crowd
No parties or socials, nothing wild, nothing loud

Life sucks at the moment there is nothing to do!

But Wait…

My glass isn't half empty but actually half full
I have a job! I am working and no longer at school

There's a roof over my head I actually have my own flat
I am surrounded with gadgets on the couch where I am sat

I have friends who all love me and family too
So what if I haven't heard from my usual crew

There is food in my tummy and I have a warm bed at night
I don't have any arguments and I don't come home to a fight

My health is quite good I have my looks and my youth
I can go out when I feel like it to tell you the truth

What was I thinking about! What a nugget, what a fool
My glass is not half empty, my glass is almost full

My Friend

Sometimes to get to where you are,
You need to learn from where you've been
Sometimes to heal your mental scars,
You feel the pain that's seldom seen

My friend I'm always here for you
To hear what may say
I'll walk and talk and wait with you
And help you find your way

Sometimes the path that maps your life
Is rarely very straight
You never see what's round the bend
Until it's way to late

My friend I'm always here for you
To help you find your way
I'll walk and talk and wait with you
And hear what you may say

Sometimes to see what's gone behind
To see your hope renewed
You need to learn from what has been
And the dream you once pursued

My friend I'm always here for you
To support you day by day
I'll walk and talk and wait with you
And help you find your way

Self-Importance

When we speak they don't hear the reality… rather just their blatant lies
A haze of self-importance surrounds them in their meager existence
And so armed with our objective views we continue to try
But they, shielded by the haze of self-importance, fight us off with little resistance
With self-congratulatory back patting and guffawing they meet behind closed doors
Congratulating each other on what they have achieved in their isolated meager existence
And memories of those approaching, armed with fresh ideas still litter the floors
But shielded by the haze of self-importance they fight them all off with little resistance

A new dawn breaks and realization sets in they are alone and cut off from this dynamic new era
The haze of self-importance clears from their meager existence
We stand tall together and unified, armed with objective views and fresh ideas
And no longer are they shielded by the haze of self-importance... they fall with little resistance

Always

I have loved you from the day we met and first became firm
friends
I listened to your joys and woes and helped your heart to mend

I am with you in your darkest days and supported you through
your wars
I am by your side for always dear at home or on distant shores

My heart and soul belong to you and through whatever life
throws our way
I will love you no matter what my dear until my dying day

My Dad

He sits in his chair and complains of the cold
Time has caught up, my dad's looking old
His memory is fleeting and he regresses to the past
He is still fighting on but how long can this last

My dad has fought wars in far hot distant lands
From the jungles of Borneo to hot dunes of sand
He sits in his chair too frail to go outside
A blank screen he watches with his dog by his side

The enemy within for years hidden from sight
Breaks free from his mind and terrorizes his night
The pills he now takes control much of this fear
His eyes unfocused filled with unshed tears

He fought for his queen, his country and our precious land
He was proud of his regiment the station they manned
He travelled far, over land, through air and over sea
And now his mind is trapped within this frail body that you see

Weather

A giggle of sunshine
A frown of fog
A shrug of a breeze
A hug of smog

Our British weather
Is an emotive feller
But makes a green and pleasant land

A roll of thunder
A wrap of mist
A touch of frost
To add to the list

Our British seasons
Are just the reason
We have a green and pleasant land

News

Looking back as the year comes to a close I reflect on what's gone on by
War and hunger, poverty and rage... I shake my head and sigh

An ever flowing river of sorrow seems to run across the land
The greed and ignorance, hatred and envy created by our own hand

But what about the tears of joy and the news that is happy and good
We never see enough of this and I honestly think we should

The negativity in all our lives should never take the lead
And equal balance if bad and good is what we really need

Doubt

Words are sometimes not enough to express what needs to be
said
Some things take a lot of time to get it right and to put it all to
bed
So many times we jump so far and our conclusions are all
wrong
The song sheets from which we all sing are just a different
song

To rush head long without a check is a silly thing to do
Falsehoods seem a matter of fact when what is said is true
Respect and trust are fragile things and cast aside with ease
And many people come across as extremely hard to please

A tunnel vision blinkered view by narrow minded twits
With snippy mails, sarcastic quotes and horrid little quips
let's take a view for a change from a few steps further out
And have some trust in what you see from within and the
world about

Friends

Twilight is a time for cheer
To eat some bread and drink some beer
A time to spend with friends alike
A hearty laugh and a friendly fight

A day in this little Town

The morning has woken wrapped up in a fuzzy blanket of mist
And an eerie silence befalls this little town
A late summer sun burns in the sky warming the afternoon up
And the blanket of mist is put by for another day in this happy
little town

Nightfall comes early and the air cools quickly as families ease
into their evening activities
And the lights go on in every home in this cosy little town
Children in pj's with squeaky clean skin are ready for bed get
snuggled down in a fuzzy blanket of warmth and dreams
And the lights all go out in this sleepy little town

Oor Laddies

Here's to the laddies – the whole array of them
they're charming and talented – each one a wee gem

Where else can one find such superior men who excel
At... well... Gossiping, eating and napping so well?

They can sing, they can dance, they can speak Burns's quotation;
Whit they're really best at is at procrastination

But let us not sell our laddies up short
For they do noble deeds of many a sort

Not one comes to mind but I am sure there's a few...
like haudin' up the bar till the morn's cast her dew

Like Rob Roy and Mel Gibson, they're brave to the core
there is nae doubt they hail from... the wild men of yore.

But whit's the source of this strength that they aw seem te have?
Is it whiskey or Buckfast or the port in their glass?

Nay dae nae be silly! it's not what's in their glass...
but its whit's at their back – their bonny wee lass!

As long as you shovel the snow fae the drive
and chop aw the wood te keep the hame fires alive.

Then the love of yer lassies you'll always sustain
and ye'll aw hae yer dinner and need never complain

Shattered Dreams?

This picture's not right
It's broken
You have taken the light
Fled into the night
You leave only a shattered dream

The sunshine has gone
It's taken
You know right from wrong
And the words to the song
You leave only my shattered dream

But my pride is intact
Fact
I will not be beaten
You will not defeat me
I will rebuild my shattered dreams

The future looks bright
There is definitely a light
You think you have won
You can't carry on
I will continue to build on my dreams.

Ties

The ties that bind us are always there
No matter what comes to pass

The ties that bind us and the friendship we share
Were always meant to last!

The ties that bind us no matter where our paths may finally go
The ties that bind us always dear, will bind us heart and soul

The ties that bind us bring us back
when we are all alone

The ties that bind us reunite us
from where ever we may roam

The ties that bound us from the start have helped us all along
The ties that bound us are always here and forever will grow
strong

Never ending...

I paint the silver linings on the clouds that have lost their shine
I care more for those who choose to careless from time to
bloody time
I feel hope for the hopeless when their hope has lost its way
And I count the hours in one day of many countless days
It is never ending

I remember uneventful moments from the past when you were full of life

I cut through the smog of adversity with the edge of an expectant knife

I start to read that never-ending story to my child who is eager to hear the end

And I amend the thread of the heartless plot to help her broken heart to mend

It seems to be never ending

But

The silver lining is never lost just stored away from time to time

And all those people who seemed to care less don't always lose their shine

The hopeless few will find their way and are never lost for long

And the countless days accounted for when we sing a brand new song

Is it never ending?

Uneventful moments add to our memories that we hold to us to dear

And adversity is a friendly force and not and enemy that hides quite near

The never ending story will end and she shall sleep without a fear

And her broken heart will always mend with my help and a friendly ear

There's always an ending.

The Hills

A magnificent sight
All dusted with white
The hills that surround oor fair land

A strong winter sun dazzles
As it reflects off the castle
And the hills that protect oor fair land

A breathtaking view
In the mist and morn's dew
And a river runs ower oor fair land

A distant beat of a drum
Some bagpipes that hum
Ancient history echoes through oor fair land

The Storm

I can see the storm approaching soon
The horizon grows quite bleak
The thunder clouds are rolling in
To put a dampener on my week

My days have gone from bad to worse
The answers hide behind the cloud
Irrational thoughts that plague my mind
And wrap me in this shroud

A heavy weight descends on me
My shoulders bear the strain
There is no sunshine in my life just now
Just dark clouds and lots of rain

From time to time I see sunshine
And my happiness I will share
My thoughts abate for a little while
But the storm is always there

A Blanket of Memories

I am knitting a blanket of memories
To warm you when you are cold
I am knitting a blanket of memories
To remind you as you grow old

Memories of your funny nan
And my quirky little ways
My yummy cakes and weird wee cat
And strange things that I say

I am knitting a blanket of memories
In shades of purple and white
I am knitting a blanket of memories
To comfort you through the night

To comfort you when you are ill
And feeling not too bright
To wrap you up and snuggle down
As the day turns into night

I am knitting a blanket of memories
To remind you when I am gone
I am knitting a blanket of memories
You remind you when you have grown

To remind you of your child hood days
And the sounds that remind you of home
Your brothers and your sister
And to say you're not alone

I am knitting you a blanket of memories
With my love entwined within it
I hope you will treasure it always
And you feel the love I've knitted into it

What is your...

What is your hug?
is it a snuggly blanket
or a warm mug of tea
is it the arms of a loved one you very seldom see?

What is your comfort
is it a hot blazing fire on a cold winters eve
is it holding your mums warm hand
up her cosy jacket sleeve?

Some people long for a hug or a squeeze
and some don't have a jacket or a warm cosy sleeve

Lets not take for granted
the pleasure that we have
lets not take for granted
the pleasure some don't have

Where is your shelter
when life goes awry
is it in a house or room
or a bed where you lay

Where is your happy place
where you retreat when you are low
is it a place or a memory
that helps you return your glow

Some people long for shelter
or a happy place to go
and some are trapped in memories
too scared to just let go

Lets not take for granted
the places that we have
lets not take for granted
what some just do not have.

My Wish

I wish I was your ray of sun that brightens up your day
I wish I was your shining star to watch you where you lay

I can't be with you all the time but I write this just to say
I wish I was right next to you when the day is just not your day

I wish I could just hug you close and wipe your tears away
I wish you could just stay a child and never age a single day

I can't be with you all the time but one day you must fly the
nest
I wish I could protect you all the time when life puts you to the
test

I wish I could tell you how it feels when you leave through my
front door
I wish I could tell you how it feels when it chills my very core

I can't be with you all the time and I can't teach you all I've
known
but you must grow and learn much more from me and the
seeds that I have sown

Me Time

We lead such busy lives these days with little time to spare
We pack so much in to our day, our time we like to share
We fit it in no matter what when others ask us to
And forget the plans that we have made for what we want to
do

But life is short and we should not waste a single moment in
the day
Live life to the full, experience it all and never lose your way
We hear these mantras preached to us when we really need
some space
We need to charge our batteries up we are human. It's not a
race

Our time is precious and yes we share but we need some time
alone
To reflect on just how far we have come and to rest a weary
bone
We need some time without them saying can you just do this
once for us
You're the only one that we can ask in you we place our trust

So when next you ask for me to do another thing for you
Remember I also have a life with other things to do
I am not being selfish I would love to help you with your job
or task
But don't be upset when I say no on occasions when you ask

Living the Dream

The Dream
Your breath is soft against my cheek
Your face is peaceful as you sleep
Your golden hair halo's your head
Your dreams are calm when you're in our bed

The Reality
Your breath it stinks what were you fed
Your snore is enough to awaken the dead
Your hair is matted to your face
And your legs they think they are in a race

The Dream
An angelic face I could watch all night
It turns out you are my Mr Right
I hug you close and hold you tight
Until the dawn and morning light

The Reality
The urge to smack you till the noise it stops
A blissful sleep! What is that? I've forgot
Your body holds the heat of hell's fires
your mutterings far from the sound of heavens choirs

The Dream
We lay entwined and watch TV
Happy in each other's company
The film is on but we don't see
Just togetherness... you and me

The Reality
We stuff our face with a TV meal
Engrossed in Noel and his Deal or no Deal
We burp and fart in harmony
Together apart just you and me

The Dream
Hand in hand we hit the town
With smile on face and not a frown
A civilised lunch or a Costa coffee
We smile and laugh with all to see

The Reality
Let's split up and get this done
There's not enough time to have any fun
A drive through burger on the way home
Then you're off on your travels, I have tea alone

Spirit

I am your Spirit, your life and your own solar flare
I erupt from your body into the surrounding air

I am your spirit, your essence and your soul
your lust for life and I keep you whole

I am what gets you started each day when you wake
I keep you going without nap or break

I am invisible to the eye but always around
forever in your presence your anchor, your ground

Grant me my freedom to show you the way
release me and love me and forever I stay

Good Afternoon

Good afternoon dear fellow how are you this afternoon
There are clouds outside and there's a coming storm
emotions are high within this little room

Good afternoon to you one and all
While we sit and ponder when the weather will warm
When the sun will rise in a fiery ball

Good afternoon I wish your day to be fine
As we are homeward bound
And our hopes set on the horizon of time

The Battle

Your outstretched arms now welcome me, and I find peace
therein at last
It has been a long hard fight you know and life's slipped by
just way to fast

Allow me to rest in your arms tonight, for I have no where left
to go
Allow me to rest in your house a while, let me rest my weary
soul

Looking back as we always do my life was not that bad
I've had some ups and downs of course, but more happy times
than sad

Allow me to rest in your arms for ever more, there is no where
I'd rather go
Allow me to rest in your house for ever more, let me rest my
weary soul

My family are here around me now as I welcome your warm
embrace
And I see the love within their hearts and soul, mirrored upon
their face

Allow me to rest in your arms a while, for I have no where left
to go
Allow me to rest in your house tonight, let me rest my weary
soul

I have made my peace with all and now I am ready to reach
for your light
I've paid my dues and I'm happy now, my world has been put
to right

Allow me to rest in your arms, there is no where I'd rather be
Allow me to rest in your house a while, I am tired from the fight you see

As I now rest my head and I find peace at last
all my dreams have been chased, fond memories past

Allow me to rest in your arms tonight, for I have no where left to go
Allow me to rest in your house a while, let me rest my weary soul

I will have peace evermore now that my race has been run
The battle is over by the setting of my sun

Stronger Now

Listen to the deafening silence within a noise filled crowded room
We see the transparencies of our deceptive friends who promise they will stay
Can you feel the empty hold it has as they leave us all too soon
And only fools with gold in grasp will offer the price we pay

The noise erupts and hurt small ears but nothing is ever said
The empty conversations linger and problems put to bed
The stories noted for future use, a memory that we'll feed
With arms and legs it grows and grows in a hundred people's heads

A translucent façade, a wall around, a barrier behind which we hide
An ineffective protector of those not wanting to take a side
A fence on which they sit between, so nothing ever needs to be a lie
A persona built of hopes all dashed and a river of tears were cried

A support, a crutch that is offered at first quickly dissolves away
The protective shield we are told to use will eventually rot and fray
Realisation that we stand alone as the light fades from the day
And in the dark we walk alone, told to make it our own way

The price is high but within in our reach of course the piper fee is fair
But goal posts move and interest applied as others want their share
The can of worms is open now and it's difficult lid to repair
Hunger is replaced by greed and is as intoxicating as the air

We now stand alone and make our way when our supporters have now all fled
And down a narrow path alone we walk where once we were led
The piper is paid and the account now closed from the sweat and tears we have all bled
And stronger now than ever before we bury the past that is now dead

Travellers Tales

I travel the world through the tales I am told
The countries that we visit and sites to behold

I travel the world with each travellers tale
A sun on their back and a wind in their sail

Each journey anew and each land that's discovered
each memory lane and image recovered

Each tale we recant and experience told
I travel along with the young and the old

My friends from afar and those who live near
each memory born and treasured so dear

You each know your place and from where you all start
keep telling your tales that imprint on my heart

The Twitter

On the tip of a tree top high up in the sky
A little bird pauses to watch others fly by

He stretches his wings and in a voice crystal clear
Tweets out is wee story to all that can hear
He sings of his journey and how far he has flown
Since flying his nest he has travelled alone

Some sights he has seen brings joy to his heart
And his voice soars with happiness as he recants from the start

Some sights fill him with sorrow and his song fades in the wind
And he sheds a wee tear for all those who have sinned

Proud of his song he flies off on the breeze
And travels onward to find other tall trees

The Ant

An ant went round and round his hill
Thinking of what to do
When he came upon an anteater
Who was looking for his shoe

Good morrow said the anteater
I seem to have lost my shoe
Can you help me find it friend
I'd be pleased of help from you

Of course the tiny ant replied
And set about the task
He looked all around his hill
To do as he was asked

Over and around the hill
The ant looked far and wide
From here to there and there to here
To across the other side

From dawn till dusk the ant searched on
But no shoe did he find
And went to tell the anteater
He hoped he did not mind

On his return he found the creature
With his tongue inside his hill
He had eaten all the ants inside
He had eaten his very fill

No shoe was found that very day
And as far as ant's concerned
Anteaters don't wear shoes
A lesson has been learned

The Hedge

A bitter wind, some driving rain
I think it looks like snow again
In staggered file right up the hill
to encounter another mindless kill

Morale is low, there're all on edge
wee Jimmy's found a comfy hedge
their eyes are peeled they lay in wait
nerves of steel, in ready state

From dusk till dawn an ambush set
the cut off crews exchange a bet
they settle in, their ground they stand
awaiting to hear a word of command

Then round the spur they filter through
the first is quite weary, the second unsure
a third and a fourth, the signal goes back
they give the all clear to the rest of the pack

The K zone, they're trapped, the team do their job
each one in that place says a prayer to their god
the recce escape to continue the story
but the tales that they tell are not about glory

Everyone loses, no battles are won
a lesson well learned when you carry a gun
how can we kill for the good of mankind?
we bury the dead, out of sight out of mind

Trophies are kept, battle honours are won
each put on display with a remarkable gun!
The nerves of steel are all shot and they're all still on edge
I remember the night I spent in that hedge

The Eagle

Gliding, soaring, flying high
Riding the thermals in the clear blue sky
Far above you watch your quarry
A skittish wee mouse so small and furry

From lofty vantage you see far and wide
In these Scottish glens nothing can hide
A majestic flight cross hill and vale
With well preened feathers in your wing and your tail

I can't help but stare at the beauty in thee
As you rest with your prey in a nearby tree
A glance here and there, before you silently go
And your off to the hills all dusted with snow

I Want

I want to paint the words you speak on an alabaster wall
I want to frame them in my heart engraved on my very soul

I want to film you in my mind so you can live in my memories
I want to cherish you always dear you mean that much to me

I want to hold your essence close for ever and a day
I want to be with you my love and this is how I pray

My heart and soul belongs to you however long it lasts
You are my future, my present day the die in which I'm cast

Pretty Little Poppy

Pretty little red poppy how beautiful you've grown
You overcome all the odds and survive where you are sown
A splendid splash of colour you brighten up the day
You're unaware of the joy you give when people pass your
way

Your strength is hidden deep within away from prying eyes
Your petals bold and delicate despite your meagre size
You overcome all the odds and survive where you are sown
 Pretty little red poppy how beautiful you've grown

You are what I want

You are what I want
To hold in my embrace
To make my dreams come true
And cause my heart to race

You are my solid rock
To keep me firmly grounded
To help me see my dreams come true
With you my life is rounded

You are my hope to carry on
To make my life so full
To help me realise my dreams
My heart is yours to rule

You are the spark within my soul
To keep me so alive
To help me brighten up your day
I will always be by your side

Our Funny Little Blonde Kid

Our funny little blonde kid
she's called a-steph-a-ee
likes nothing more to streak about
in just her red wellies

She has her oats for breakfast
to fuel her through to tea
our funny little blonde kid
we call her steph-a-ee

Our funny little blonde kid
her face is all aglow
she likes nothing more to entertain
and puts on quite a show

She is a little comic
she lets her giggles flow
our funny little blonde kid
just see her wee cheeks glow

Our funny little blonde kid
goes racing through the crowd
her tippee cup and skirt hitched up
she makes us laugh out loud

She loves to sing and dance for us
and makes us all feel proud
our funny little blonde kid
is entertaining to the crowd

Our funny little blonde kid
an angel you would insist
but do her wrong and it won't be long
she turns into Chukkie's sis

her evil eye will make you cry
and her hex on you won't miss
our funny little blonde kid
is not always an angelic sis

What is a Giggle?

A giggle is a wiggle of a sound that escaped my mouth
It started in my tummy and went north instead of south

It was a thought that crossed my mind re something that you
said
It went round and round until it found the way out of my
head

A giggle is a wiggle of sound that caused a little stir
And if you mind I will go and find somewhere to release it
sir

Fashion Statement

Fashion, it's a statement, A fabric war that we declare
It makes us feel like superstars or makes others stop and stare

If we are followers or leaders it's an ever changing trend
A label that says who we are, the message we like to send

Look closely at all those around, what clothes adorn their frame
Can we see the individuals, Or are they all the same?

Some are dedicated followers, the designers they adore
And some prefer just to wear, whatever's cheapest in their store

Fashion is so personal and you shouldn't dress to trend
not to line the pockets of designers or just to please a friend

You should dress with what you like from bottom through to top, be that from a unique boutique or just a charity shop

Leopard print from head to toe, quite scary don't you think?
Others like to set their sights on luminescent pink.

Granny in her safe twinset with pearls around her neck
And plastic hikers in cargo pants and boots not fit to trek

There are the Goths all dressed in black and metal in their face
Or orange ducks in thick makeup, waddling a stiletto footed race

Who are we to judge their choice it makes us who we are
It matters not if we're haute couture or a Westwood rising star

My nana often used to say that clothes should suit the wearer
It has nowt to do with me or you we shouldn't dress to please
the stare'er

(Stanza five and six were added by my good friend Alan Birdsworth – thank you Alan for your input.)

The Scars on my heart

Time passes by and memories fade
but the scars you left on my heart remain as freshly made

Time passes by and my wounds will undoubtedly heal
but the scars you left on my heart I will always and forever feel

Time passes by and from the day that we first met
the scars you carved on my heart started to heal the day you
left

Time passes by and my trust remains still shaken
but scars you left on my heart leaves my emotions shattered
and broken

Time has now passed by and our lives separately move on
and the rawness of these wounds has almost faded and gone

Time has now passed on and my life has started anew
and the memories fade of all the hurt that was caused by you

Time has now passed on and I have learned to love again
and with all of my former life with you, in my past they will
remain

Time has now passed on and I will never mourn that life you
see as my chains have all now broken and I will forever be set
free

Pretty Little Flutterby

You morphed from a little caterpillar inching across the ground
You bide your time in leafy litter munching everything around
A cocoon you spin yourself and you hide for your transformation
You re-enter the world, letting your wings uncurl with your beautiful re-creation

You are a pretty little flutterby with wings so bright and blue
You're off to visit lots of plants some old and some so new
The gentle flutter of your wings as you settle on your goal
You bring the sunshine to my heart it warms my very soul

You're a pretty little flutterby I see your vibrant sheen
Of all the insects in the land you really are the queen
So beautiful, resplendent a majestic sight to see
You gracefully flit around your land so beautiful and carefree

Your past is now forgotten a new life ahead of you
You drink your fill from the flowers around and early morning dew
This change is of your making you did this by yourself
And I thank you for all you do to bring such beauty to my life

Silent Worship

Heads all bowed as we hurry on worshipping the tiny screened device
Toddlers mimicking from an early age this new religion or vice

Sidewalks filled with fellow slaves as we snake along to our destination
The sermon today depends on our vice and we drink it without hesitation

Technology takes hold like an addictive drug that we cannot do without
God forbid if the battery runs too low and like a child we scream and we shout

The media know few do without the poison on which we are hooked
As live feeds stream to our machines and we are tweeted, chatted or just facebooked

People in groups out for the night sit together in silent prayer
quietly chat about somebody's cat and send it on to each through "share"

Have we forgotten to speak to each other to raise our heads in acknowledgement
A brief hello, a smile... you know... the way a comment used to be sent

Eyes Wide Shut

I open my eyes and what do I see
Lots of people around about me
Is it a city or is it a town
With lots of tall buildings from the sky to the ground

The people they scurry from point 'a' to point 'b'
They have little interest in you or in me
Their eyes are wide shut and see nothing around
Their journey is programmed; they have no vision or sound

I could be just like all of those people around
But I choose to look up
And see more than just ground

I open my eyes and look what I found
There are trees growing up to the sky from the ground
The flowers are blooming in all colours you see
There are insects abundant from the ant to the bee

The people who scurry miss all of this beauty
They rush around and call it their duty
Their eyes are wide shut and see nothing around
Nothing at all in sky or on ground

I could be just like all of those people around
But I choose to look up
And see more than just ground

Hills and Glens

Our journey now starts as the new sun dawns
And we settle in on our way
Excitement is building, a mystery tour
Let's see what evolves through our day

An army of silent white sentinels
Stand alone on the side of a hill
Arms rising in perpetual salute to the wind
In their duty they are never to be still

The shaven pale hills with their broken trees
Where great forests once proudly stood
Reduced to organised piles of logs
Waiting ready for our varnished planks of wood

As we journey on and the small hills grow
And around mountain spurs the road bends
Giant guardians of the glens are watching us now
Are we foe or are we new friends

The mountains open out to a valley and some lochs
And I am sure the history can almost be heard,
Breathing life into the imagery we imagine therein
Of the ancient stories we are told and we have shared

I am sure I can hear the cry of the warriors
Across the high peaks and low glens
Echoes of the past clannish gatherings
Welcoming their family and friends

In my mind I can see them all here
Assembled together on high
And I loose myself to the dream of it all
Watching the hills grow to the sky

We pass the glens of bracken and gorse
Dotted with pods of cotton wool sheep
And the vibrant velvet hills of heather
Naturally growing so wild and waist deep

The sun now dips in the dusky pink sky
And we start on our homeward road
We say goodbye to the warriors now
And the stories they have told

Good Afternoon

Good afternoon my good friend how are you this afternoon
There are clouds outside and a coming storm
emotions are high within this little room

Good afternoon to you one and all
While we sit and ponder when the weather will warm
When the sun will rise in a fiery ball

Good afternoon I wish your day to be fine
As we are homeward bound
And our hopes set on the horizon of time

The Evil Dark Overlord

The evil dark overlord with the brown curly hair
has a cheeky wee smile and a Paddington Bear stare

She will shush anything into silence when Tink is on TV
and run riot through the flat annoying anyone with glee

The evil dark overloard with the brown curly hair
will chase her brothers and sister to see what they can share

Her appetite is amazing and will eat anything in sight
and with a cheeky little grin she gives a cat treat a testing bite

The evil dark overlord with the brown curly hair
is curled up in her dressing gown so angelic on the chair

She has taken over the universe chasing aliens into submission
and after her bath, she has relaxed in front of the television

Steeeeve

He stops, you now have his full attention
He is completely still, his eye's fixed in your direction

A quick look round, his tail gives a slight flick
As he picks up his toy, a white plastic stick

He presents you his prize and the look says "let's play"
"I've been locked up alone in this flat all bloody day"

He leaps up to catch it with such agility and speed
Then grace is forgotten as he lands on his hied

He loses his stick but brings a bobble instead
But after an hour and a half decides he wants fed

After a head bump and cuddle he curls up in your lap
Tired out from his play he takes a wee nap

Answers that elude us

It's not what's said, explanations we're fed,
but something we no longer recall
It's not what we know from this political show
no lessons from a previous fall

answers that elude us
answers never found
answers not even hidden
in these journals leather bound

it's not what is recanted periodically by
those who know best
it's not our cumulative knowledge
that will win when it comes to the test

answers that elude us
answers can be found
answers not even hidden
in these journals leather bound

questions have been asked before
lessons we were taught
the answers found to questions asked
we had what now is sought

answers that elude us
answers have been found
answers that were hidden
not just in these journals bound

It may not be the key we hold
that unlocks that which is sought
it may just be that what we ask
is not what we purport

answers may elude us
answers have been found
answers that weren't hidden
not in these journals bound

Cut Off

I feel lonely in your company
I am cut off like others around you
You feel lonely in their company
If only they knew you

You have seen the world at its most depraved
And still you carry on
You wish those sights were never seen
The terror that went on

I feel lonely in your company
You're cut off again from those around you
You feel lonely in their company
If they only really knew

You have fought the wars the news reports
To the media every day
You have fought the daemons ever since
You cope in your own way

I feel lonely in your company
Please let me help you through the dark
You feel lonely in our company
But there is light albeit just a spark

Up Up and Away

Layla felt so very sad
It made her want to cry
Layla whispered to her dad
"I fear I cannot fly"

Now don't you fear oh chick of mine
Your feathers need to grow
You need more patients and in time
Your fluffy down will go

Your wings grow strong with each new day
And your plumes will start to shine
Believe me chick when daddy says
You will fly if given time

Layla tried so very hard
She flapped her wings in vain
Each day she tried in her front yard
Then up and down the lane

She tried all kinds of different things
As her feathers slowly grew
And as she flapped her lovely wings
Her hopes and dreams renewed

In the park a child ran by
His balloons escaped his grasp
They floated up into the sky
Layla jumped as they went past

As she tried to grab them in her beak
She flapped her wings so very fast
And gathered up a little speed
Layla caught them with one last gasp

Layla took a look around
A gasp of joy oh my
Her feet were no longer on the ground
As she rose higher in the sky

The drama now all over she went to tell her dad
He could see her teary eyes
But Layla was no longer sad
She said "I am a chicken and I can fly"

Easter Bonnet

A bright sunny day down Puddlepond Lane
Henrietta was all of a tizz

Her new Easter Bonnet has a little bee on it
And she can hear it go bzz bzz bzz

Oh what shall we do the parade is about due
And I don't have a moment to spare

I don't want to harm you or even alarm you
I haven't anything else I can wear

But after a while the bee flew off with a smile
And thanked her for use of her hat

I had to come see said the little buzzy bee
You bonnet's like a flowery mat

She smiled at the bee can I offer you some tea
I have a few minutes to spare

I thank you but no I really must go
And flew up with a buzz in the air

Laughter and Tears

Memories of when you were wee
The laughter and tears upon my knee
The stress of school, the fights with friends
Keeping up with the latest trends

In the playground sharing toys
Then suddenly... there were boys!
The crying when they broke your heart
But soon forgotten, reboot, restart

The first few years in your own wee home
And now I look back at how much you've grown
A lifetime now gone, it's all a memory
From the laughter and tears upon my knee

A Little Cottage

A little cottage by the sea
A holiday with the family
Waves gently lapping at the shore
The sun is shining, can't want for more

A bimble over rocky pools
With fishing nets, such handy tools
Watch your feet its slippy here
You wouldn't want a soggy rear

The younger ones want to dive right in
Aarron leads and we watch him swim
Amazed we watch him open mouthed
The rest jump in then right back out

Fergus leading all astray
Look at him leading the way
Never watching where he stands
Ends up wet from where he lands

Sitting out front watching the various sports
Wishing we had brought some shorts
The sun dips down in our little bay
What a wonderfully perfect end to the day

Easter Fay

Easter time fills Fay with glee
as bunnies hide treats for all to see

She watches children as they have fun
finding Easter eggs in the morning sun

Their baskets fill with chocolate sweets
and other delightful little treats

Fey

Fey lived in the meadow close to Puddlepond Lane
She liked to play in the sunshine and dance in the rain
She liked to fly on a breeze with her pretty little wings
And lay in the grass as the nightingale sings

What is Christmas

We save all year round to buy you good cheer
To bestow all our gifts on those we hold dear
The worry and stress in a hope we chose right
And that the gift that we buy does not start a fight

But what is the point it's no longer so clear
The ring of the cash tills is all we can hear
The queues that have formed for the toy that sold out
Is this what the festive celebration is about?

In the world that we all live in are we expecting too much?
Is it all about parties, eating, drinking and such?
We seem to have forgotten what it's really about
Do I need to remind you? Do you need me to SHOUT?

It's about a small baby born a long time ago
Who changed the whole world with the stories he told
He taught us to be thankful for all that we are
It all started with three men who followed a star

Born in a manger when the inns were all full
During a great census when King Herod was in rule
The gifts that were given was just once at his birth
To do him the lifetime he spent on this earth

The celebration then was short and it was sweet
To honor the savior wrapped up in a sheet
When our hopes were all placed in the hands of a child
Our savior was born so meek and so mild

The lessons he taught in the centuries gone by
Handed down through the years from the baby's first cry
The gifts he received, myrrh, frankincense and gold
So let us remember the story he told

Choices

I can show you a path
but you must find your own way
I can show you the dawn
but what will you do with the day

I can offer you a choice
but you need to choose
I can offer you my friendship
what is there to lose?

I can tell you a story
are you ready to listen
I can tell you to stop
will that stop your mission

I can give you a penny
would you give me your thought
I can give a clue
will it find what is sought

I can do what I can
I am only one voice
I can be in your life
but it's only your choice

Regret

A change that we didn't make
A word we left unsaid
The memories we kept alive
That we should have put to bed

Temptation

The things that whisper through my mind subtle and suggestive
The things that whisper through my mind causing me to question

The things that whisper through my mind ignite the fires within
The things that whisper through my mind adventures to begin

The things that whisper through my mind I ignore from time to time
The things that whisper through my mind I am forced to leave behind

The things that whisper through my mind that threaten the status quo
The things that whisper through my mind I am told I must outgrow

The things that whisper through my mind are silly but exciting
The things that whisper through my mind are comforting and a little frightening

The things that whisper through my mind temptation proves too much
The things that whisper through my mind trampled under sensibilities crutch

The things that whisper through my mind beckons with a seductive tug
The things that whisper through my mind addictive as a drug

The things that whisper through my mind says be yourself one day
The things that whisper through my mind says ignore what haters say

The things that whisper through my mind says dance and laugh and sing
The things that whisper through my mind says feel the joy it brings

The things that whisper through my mind says be brave and grasp a hold
The things that whisper through my mind says let your life unfold

Nature signals change

Nature signals that change is due
Seasons move from old to new
Summer with her leaves of green
Now steps aside for the autumn scene

Golden browns and fiery reds
And bobble hats upon our heads
Misty breath escapes our lips
And frosty tingly finger tips

Bonfires blaze at the start of November
Then another date we respect and remember
Pretty soon the new is now old
Then another story can be told

Dawn

Her hair whipped gently around her face
As she gazed far out to sea
Her mind was in another place
A place she used to be

Flickered memories like movie stills
As the sun begins to rise
A void within her starts to fill
As she begins to realize

The darkness turns at the break of dawn
And light paints the morning skies
A strength renewed that was once gone
The happiness fills her eyes

A new resolve embraced her soul
As the dawn breaks the bright new day
The picture now complete and whole
The sunshine lights her way

What's inside your head?

I wonder about you and what's in your head
The words you don't say, the discussions unsaid

What are you thinking when I catch your gaze on me
Across the crowded floor or when we're watching TV

I feel your eyes fall upon me as I go to leave a room
A smile or frown across your brow as I sing a familiar tune

Occasionally a smile escapes, its reflection in your eyes
You try to hide it quickly as I catch it by surprise

This silence isn't golden and traps you inside yourself
It keeps us from our happiness and will destroy your mental
health

We need to learn to talk again the way it used to be
And share the things that makes you smile just between us, just
you and me

Open your Eyes

I open my eyes and what do I see
Lots of people around about me
Is it a city or is it a town
With lots of tall buildings from the sky to the ground

The people they scurry from point 'a' to point 'b'
They have little interest in you or in me
Their eyes are wide shut and see nothing around
Their journey is programmed; they have no vision or sound

I could be just like all of those people around
But I choose to look up
And see more than just ground

I open my eyes and look what I found
There are trees growing up to the sky from the ground
The flowers are blooming in all colours you see
There are insects abundant from the ant to the bee

The people who scurry miss all of this beauty
They rush around and call it their duty
Their eyes are wide shut and see nothing around
Nothing at all in sky or on ground

I could be just like all of those people around
But I choose to look up
And see more than just ground

A Pen

A pen can put the world to rights
But start so many wars
A pen can start so many fights
Yet open many doors

A pen can mask the writers face
When they hide behind their words
Can make or break the best of them
A double sided sword

A pen can woo the coldest heart
Light a fire in your soul
A pen can freeze the fires of hell
And cause the mighty ones to fall

A pen can write romantic verse
Or a story for a child
Pen lyrics to a rock ballad
Cause halos to slip and slide

A mighty weapon the pen and ink
To bring countries to their knees
But also calm the troubled lands
Sign treaties to bring world peace

Tangled

A tangled knot was sat one day
unable to do… well not much!
It spent its life so intertwined
Intimate with all it touched

Its life was never all its own
And others knew it too
The gossiping, the accusations
It was like living in a zoo

Bright one morn it awoke to find
Alone and bereft from all
Straightened out it starts anew
Sets out to have a ball

Pretty soon it meets someone
To join its party life
Then one by one more join the fun
Another tangled night…

Another Chapter

My story spans so many years
I've had lots of laughs and shed some tears
My story takes me through many changes
Making new friends by speaking to strangers

A chapter closed and I recall things that I have done
The many battles I have lost and the wars that I have won
My humble start oooh way back when I was wet behind the ears
I have seen them all they come and go over twenty odd long years

I've learned so many things from them, the leaders that did not last
Some good some bad but all will stay a memory of my past
The kids that come and go they grow so fast before my eyes
Privileged to meet each one and guide them in their lives

Lessons learned and skills acquired will help in years to come
And now it's time and retirement calls my duty has been done
I will remember fondly this chapter in my kaleidoscopic life
The many characters I have met they joys the woes the strife

One last thing that I must say to all the friends I've made
The chapter cannot close just yet until a tribute has been made
I've done my best and made them proud at all that I have done
And thank you all who had faith in me and made my cadet time fun

The Track of Life

I am on the single track of life
And I walk the unyielding line
It's pretty clear what I'm to do
Sometime dust obscures the way

The track is there from day one
Until the day I die
It's pretty clear what I'm to do
Some dust gets in my eyes

I try to look for alternatives
My journey's already set
It's pretty clear what I'm to do
I take what I can get

Mum knows best is what they say
Big brothers watching you
It's pretty clear what lies ahead
I do what I must do

Focus on the nine to five
You work to get ahead
It's pretty clear I need to live
Retirement when your dead

The family average one point eight
Statistics give us a steer
It's pretty clear where I am
The dusty track now clear

But just supposing the track now ends
And the journey incomplete
Is it clear what the next step is
The plan is a new blank sheet

Can I be the master of my track
Does my journey have to end
It's clear the powers that rule
Fear the winds that make them bend

The Report

PXR is written down this report that must be sent
To document our doings and just how the training went
It's the first I've ever written so my time was carefully spent
Setting out the subject headers making clear on what is meant

In **General** we let you know the purpose of this literary piece
An opening description about the course in this a post release
Honesty is what is called, we do not want to fleece
Tell it how it is my boy - Christ it's like talking to the police

Our **aim** is clear when it's all laid out, about what we're going to do
On why and what we are doing here, our promise from me to you
You will be taught what is required and you may not have a clue
The hoops we jump to deliver this is clear to just a few

Our **objective** makes it clear on what we want to be achieved

"What all the students passed the course! – if that's what's to be believed!"
"Will you really fulfil your stated goal? will the losers also succeed?"
Your negativity will not last long when you see them stop your bleed!

So **Personnel and admin** we report, the finer details told
The ADS know what needs done and venture out into the cold
They clean the kit until it shines and report when they find mould
The staff were all fantastic they look just like they just won gold

The scarlet pimpernel is somewhere about this training place
But if you need him when you want him you need to tag his ass to trace
At start and at finish he will deem to show his elusive little face
And everything will be okay have faith in our human race

With **Safety and security** we cannot forget the golden rule
A system safe for training needs to be clear to every fool
A verbal picture is painted now it's like being back at school
Assessments done and printed out, no one tried to pull the wool

Logistics now is where we are and added to the list
Location was quite central too up north behind scotch mist
Our food and menus unusually good we could not shake a fist
Fresh fruit and veg upon the plate the cook we could have kissed

As usual the **training stores** we found where not as how we left
And items needed for the course had seemed to gone adrift
So through our kit we had a look to give our stores a lift
And carried on regardless even though a little miffed!

Accommodation pros and cons we need to add them too
We inspected every room we used and even checked the loo
The showers seems a little bonkers some so hot they boil and stew
The heating poles apart as well it may need to be renewed

Training went all as planned the students had some fun
They started at the break of dawn and past the setting of the sun
A lot of hours and lessons learned with prizes to be won
The team were all on the ball they just got the jobs all done

To **summarize** the events for you no need to read the score
The training was a great success regardless to our store
A happy team that worked quite well whom the students all adore
You should be happy as a pig in shit with first aid blood and gore

Your duty is done

You see the pride and loyalty of all those who've gone before
The values and standards instilled in you along with so much
more
The regimental history bound within your family tree
Following in your father's footsteps as you train for what will
be

So stand down soldier your duty is done
the battle is over the war has been won

You fight the wars that you are ordered to without a hesitant
pause
You train and travel all around the world to help a worthy
cause
Your bag is packed and you leave behind the family you hold
so dear
To help restore some peace to those who have lived so long in
fear

So stand down soldier your duty is done
the battle is over the war has been won

You be the best, have trained the rest, you do all you can
And standing proud amongst the rest you help your fellow man
You ensure the family name goes on within the regimental role
Your place is there amongst them all the brave the proud and
bold

So stand down soldier your duty is done
the battle is over the war has been won

Mine is bigger than yours

My toy is better than your toy
It cost my dad a bob or two
My toy is bigger than your toy
And available to a privileged few

Your toy is bigger than my toy
But bigger is not always better
Your toy is a limited offer
But I am not really a trend setter

My dad is bigger than your dad
Just look at all he can do
My dad is better than your dad
When he comes home I will show you it's true

My dad may not be bigger than your dad
And he is certainly not the worst
My dad may not be better than your dad
But his family will always come first

My castle is bigger than your castle
So I am the boss of you
My castle is better than your castle
Accessible to a privileged few

Your castle is bigger than my castle
And it has an impressive throne
But my castle is open to everyone
And I like to call it my home

My army is better than your army
Just look how many battles we have won
My army is bigger than your army
I will prove it with my shiny new gun

Your army may be better than my army
But war is not my ultimate goal
Your gun may be big and shiny
But will never capture my freedom or soul

Spirit

I am your spirit, your life and your own solar flare
I erupt from your body into the surrounding air

I am your spirit, your essence and your soul
your lust for life and I keep you whole

I am what gets you started each day when you wake
I keep you going without nap or break

I am invisible to the eye but always around
forever in your presence your anchor, your ground

Grant me my freedom to show you the way
release me and love me and forever I stay

My Beautiful Freak

I can feel for your pain, life can be so bitterly cruel
Your pride is all battered, and you feel like a fool

He gave you some hope and you felt so alive
Happiness fulfilled as you stood by his side

But you had an adventure and experienced new things
Your life took a turn as you spread open your wings

You travelled afar in this journey of yours
Discovered new roads and you opened new doors

All is not lost and just look what you gained
You experienced a new world and some lovely new friends

You have learned about you and the talents you hold
You are fun and vivacious, so beautiful and bold

You found he was not Mr Right after all
He was just Mr Right-now, a handy "on call"

Have heart and have hope, let your spirit go free
Open your mind as it's important to see

You will find your true mate in the most unlikely of places
He will stare back at you from a sea of new faces

Life makes it hard to find the perfection we seek
be patient my friend my beautiful freak x

Silent Worship

Heads all bowed as we hurry on worshipping the tiny screened device
Toddlers mimicking form an early age this new religion or vice

Sidewalks filled with fellow slaves as we snake along to our destination
The sermon today depends on our vice and we drink it without hesitation

Technology takes hold like an addictive drug and we cannot do without
god forbid if the battery runs too low and like a child we scream and we shout

The media know few do without the poison on which we are hooked
As live feeds streamed to our machines and we are tweeted, chatted or just facebooked

People in groups out for the night sit together in silent prayer
quietly chat about somebody's cat and send it on to each through "share"

Have we forgotten to speak to each other to raise our heads in acknowledgement
A brief hello, a smile … you know … the way a comment used to be sent

Making my stand

You're stupid, you're ignorant what possessed me to make you
my wife
You're useless you're worthless you're a burden, a thorn in
my life

I smile, he's in a good mood, and today is going to be a good
day
I have cleaned and I have polished and I know he likes it that
way

This is a pig sty, not fit to live in, how can I bring my friends
around here
You're an embarrassment, just look at you, no wonder they all
steer clear

It's a compliment, I have pleased him, I try not to attract their
attention
He loves me, he adores me, and so to hurt me is not his
intention

I'm sorry, it was an accident, but you made me do that to you
my dear
You're frustrating, you're clumsy, and how could you not see
that the way was not clear

I'm okay honestly, it's just a small bruise, how clumsy of me
to fall over that way
He caught me, he saved me, I am sure the marks on my arm
will soon fade away

You cooked this? It's edible!… Not the slop that you usually serve
Who taught you, have they been here, how dare you, you do have some nerve

He likes it, I am happy I pass him over mine on a clean plate
I don't need it, he likes it and he did say I needed to lose a little weight

What's wrong with you, you keep crying I remember when you used to smile
You should be happy, I love you, if you're lucky I will keep you around for a while

See he loves me! I am happy! I will smile for him all of this day
I will dress the way he likes me to and do whatever he might say

You hussy you harlot, who the hell are you trying to impress
Is he local? is he next door? I am not worried as I doubt he even exists

Where am I? There's no shouting! Why is that nurse holding on to my hand
What's she saying? That I am safe now, I was brave to finally make my stand

Me Time

We lead such busy lives these days with little time to spare
We pack so much in to our day, our time we like to share
We fit it in no matter what when others ask us to
And forget the plans that we have made for what we want to
do

But life is short and we should not waste a single moment in
the day
Live life to the full, experience it all and never lose your way
We hear these mantras preached to us when we really need
some space
We need to charge our batteries up we are human. It's not a
race

Our time is precious and yes we share but we need some time
alone
To reflect on just how far we have come and to rest a weary
bone
We need some time without them saying can you just do this
once for us
You're the only one that we can ask in you we place our trust

So when next you ask for me to do another thing for you
Remember I also have a life with other things to do
I am not being selfish I would love to help you with your job
or task
But don't be upset when I say no on occasions when you ask

Where is Summer?

Spring is round the corner
and summer's not far away
soon the sun will be bright and warm
then we can go and play

Winter has been with us
for what seem to be a while
I cannot wait to lose my coat
it makes me want to smile

We need some rain just now and then
it helps our crops to grow
and I love the sunny winter days
when the land is iced with snow

Each season has it place
and must stay a while you see
but it seems to be so long ago
that we last saw greenery

I long to feel the sun's warm rays
across my arms and face
I've had enough of rain and sleet
or the winter's biting brace

So with sunshine round the corner
hope rises in my heart
Winter takes a well-earned rest
now spring is due to start

Lest We Forget

The day is new
Repetition a must
From morning dew
To the evening dusk

Fleeting smile
As a stranger passes
I rest a while
And adjust my glasses

Another time
Another land
A single line…
A supporting hand

With help I rise
On parade I stand
Remembrance of those
Who fought for our land

They fell at my side
On a terrible day
For their country they died
What more can I say

My brothers in arms
They never grow old
Protected from harm
Their bravery told

A day every year
On parade we stand tall
A silence we hear
In respect to you all

Lest we forget…

Media Sheep

They watch with interest through undiscerning eyes
They all say their piece with silent cries
They listen to what has already been said
And nothing is heard inside of their head

Captivated only by their selfish desires
Trapped in a net of powerful wires
Led by hypocrisy they have been fed day by day
 And social media gladly paving the way

Liked and sent any re-tweeted chirp
Snowballing onward with the help of these twirps
What is the reality behind all this tripe
Is there any truth behind what they write

Warnings abundant be mindful with what you say
If the source is unknown another mind is at play
Knowing the root of what has been said
Will highlight who leads and who has been led

Guest Writers

Poems and notes from friends and family

Amanda Gillespie

Thought I would take a leaf out of my mum's book and share one of my poems, my mum is a lot better at it than me, as I am still practicing so don't laugh.

KIDS

I scrub the walls of fingerprints
pick up the mounds of clothes
I sweep the dirt that shoes track in
I wish I could use a hose

meals are served from dawn to dark
dirty dishes crowd the sink
and when they are all put away
everyone wants a drink

the washer pulls dirt and grime
from jeans worn thin and patched
they look so very neat and clean
yuck! just look at what the pockets have hatched

blistering bumps and bloody knees
I should have been a nurse
I take it all in shaky stride
just grateful it's not worse

screams, shouts and arguments
test the keeping of my cool
stay on mums good side
is the number one rule

a soothing bath is ecstasy
a reward at the end of my rope
raising kids isn't really that bad
but first I must wash the soap

a rose can say 'I love you'
orchids can enthrall
but a weedy bouquet in a chubby fist
oh! my! that says it all

Yo Bro

we thought of you with love today
but that is nothing new
we thought of you yesterday
and the day before that too

we think of you in silence
we often speak your name
now all we have is memories
and your picture in a frame

your memory is our keepsake
with which we will never part
heaven has you in its keep
we have you in our heart

Two boys, two brothers

There are two boys in my house with Spiderman shoes
there's in the night garden with the tombiliboo's

there's bob he's a builder and Thomas the train
there's waterproof coats to wear in the rain

there's wrestling matches that turn into wars
and they both hide when it comes to their chores

There's dirt on their faces as well as their clothes
grass stain on their knees and oose between their toes

There's bath time at night with two boys to scrub
and when we're all done there's dirt round the tub

There's plasters and bruises and curious bumps
there's smile and laughter and sometimes there's grumps

There's odours most icky and booger's so green
there's more yuckier thing than I have ever seen

There's cars and there's trains and books about trucks
there's bouncy rubber balls and squeaky yellow bath ducks

Sometime they are bugs and sometimes they are frogs
sometimes they are lion's, dino's and dog's

There are cute pinstriped jackets and darling neckties
dragged right through the mud 'oh what a surprise'

There's climbing high and toppled falling
with angry tears and brotherly brawling

There's breakfast and lunchtime and dinnertime fights
there is toys in bed and tactical manoeuvres at night

There's late night whispers about plans concealing
there's creeping about and catching them stealing

There's tantrums and timeouts and extra loud noise
there's love in my house shaped like two little boys

Stephanie Gillespie

Proud

I was not there to help you then
a year ago today
I want to hug your pain away
I just don't know what to say

I see you thinking back to then
and it always gets you down
so I have made a special book for you
to make a smile from your worried frown

This book is full of happiness
to remind you when your blue
the friends who like to say some words
and are all so proud of you

Beep Beep Beep

Beep beep beep breaks the silence of the room

It quickens and slows then the beep beep beep resumes
A twitch, a shiver an occasional moan adds to the tune

Lying so helpless in a world of his own
On his hospital bed in his faded white gown

What little that was there seems like its fading too fast
What little there was is not going to last

So many drips and tubes it is difficult you see
But it is his lifeline his doctor says that his body sorely needs

Without that beep beep beep would it all be so really scary
Without that beep beep beep he won't be still with you and me

By A Shy Friend

A Naughty Thought

Is it okay to have a naughty thought, what message does it send
Is it okay to have them about my company, a colleague or a
friend
Is it okay to have these thoughts to what actions would they
lend
Is it okay to have those thoughts or is it something that has to
end

Is it okay to have naughty thoughts while walking down the
street
Is it okay to have those thoughts of strangers I pass or meet
Is it okay to have a thought about the ladies I'd like to charm
Is it okay to have those thoughts and does it do me any harm

It is okay to have naughty thoughts whatever time or place
They help to put a spring in my step and a smile upon my face
It is okay to have these thoughts as my thoughts are there to
amuse
It is okay to have these thoughts about anything I choose

My thoughts are hidden deep within and no one has a clue
They may be about anything they may be all about you
A thought is an action not acted upon and a thought they will
remain
An un-acted thought is a personal thing and keeps be balanced
and sane

Short Story

This is a short story I used to tell my daughters at bed time when they were small.

The Mountain

A long time ago in the middle of a crystal clear ocean there was a small island.

In the middle of this island there was an enormous mountain that reached high into the sky. The mountain was so big that the top of it disappeared into the fluffy white clouds that hung around its many peaks like balls of white candy floss.

A lush green forest ringed the base of the mountain and it melted away into the sandy beach lapped by the warm waters of the ocean.

The island was inhabited by a tribe of people who were happy and content with their simple lives. Many of the people on the island thought their happiness was due to the spirit of the island that lived in the heart of mountain. The spirit gave the mountain magical powers and that these magical powers were responsible for the love, peace and harmony that the people on the island had enjoyed for thousands of years.

The people lived in small groups dotted around the island. They worked very hard every day and helped one another if anyone was found to struggle even a little bit.

Every year, just as the weather turned a bit cooler, the people on the island gathered around the north side of the mountain where the stars seem to shine the brightest and when a deep carpet of tiny white flowers bloomed just for the occasion. On this special day everyone would bring gifts for the spirit to thank her for the peace and harmony on the island. They would offer prayers, sing songs of their ancestors and ask her to speak to the spirit of the sky and ask him bring back the warm days soon.

Near the opening to a deep cavern there was a smooth flat plateau. The stone sparkled like the stars in the sky and the people believed that the spirits of the mountain and sky sat together to discuss heavenly secrets.

Prayers were often whispered and secret wishes were written on small pieces of paper and placed in a small hollow close by the plateau for the spirits to read. As each message was left the people would rub the smooth rock to give thanks to the spirit for all they have. They would walk away with a warm happy glow inside that made them feel calm and happy, their hearts filled with hope that their wishes will be answered.

After visiting the sacred plateau the people on the island would be so happy that they went back home and decorated their homes with brightly coloured flowers and shells and prepared lots of lovely food to share with everyone on the island at a banquet later.

The island spirit was pleased to see the islanders so happy that she granted their secret requests. She also spoke to the spirit of the sky to ask for the warmer weather to return to the island soon.

Within just a few weeks the weather became much warmer. Those who wished for their fields of crops to flourish were not disappointed and anyone who wished for better health and happiness were also granted their wishes.

The island bloomed as the warm sunshine pushed the dark rain clouds away and everyone was happy.

The spirit of the island also liked to give gifts as a special thank you to anyone who was particularly kind and helpful.

The spirit placed a small piece of rock from deep inside her mountain into the darkest corner of each of their homes. As the darkness fell each evenings this special piece of rock would reflect the light from the persons kind soul and the stars in the night sky to brighten up the dark corner with a warm sparkly glow.

The island spirit only ever gave away a few of these special rocks as you needed to be very kind and helpful to receive her special gift.

The glow from the rock was so beautiful and warm that everyone wanted one.

Soon the messages left by the island people included long lists of good deeds they had done to prove to the island spirit that they had been extra nice and so were worthy of one of her special gifts, but the island spirit ignored these requests as kindness should only be given freely and not in hope of a reward.

After a few years' people noticed that the island spirit no longer gave out her gifts and they became angry. They felt that they deserved what others had been given so demanded even more that they should have a special rock. As their resentment grew they soon stopped sharing, giving and loving and they all started to squabble and fight amongst themselves, jealous of others who had been given a special gift. They bullied these people for being favoured by the spirit, calling them names and making their lives very sad.

As time went on some of the jealous people even started to take small rocks from around the base of the mountain to have for their own after they had left their annual offerings and while these rocks did glow a little they did not have the inner light of a kind soul to enhance them and were not as bright as the ones given freely by the island spirit.

Over the years people eventually started breaking pieces off the mountain, happy to have just a small piece of magical rock. Some evens started selling these "magical rocks" to people on other islands in exchange for new clothes or jewellery and a few of the greedier people even built new homes from larger pieces of rock they had carved out of the mountain.

Soon the mountain started to shrink in size as more and more people were helping themselves to pieces of it and the island spirit became very sad. She retreated deep into the depths of the mountain and hid away from all the greed and anger. Her sadness caused the island in turn to lose its magic over time and even her special gifts only glowed occasionally when an extra special deed of kindness occurred. People began to forget about the spirit but their anger, cruelty and jealousy remained for ever more

The island still lies in the middle of a crystal clear ocean somewhere but it no longer has an enormous mountain in the middle of it.

There are still people living on the island and some still have the rocks the island spirit gifted their ancestors many years ago but now they only glow when an act of unprompted kindness happens around the same time the weather turns a bit cooler and a deep carpet of tiny white flowers grows over a long forgotten cavern in what is left of the mountain.